A Nc•

a compelling program for beginning readers, designed in conjunction with leading literacy experts, including Dr. Linda Gambrell, Professor of Education at Clemson University. Dr. Gambrell has served as President of the National Reading Conference and the College Reading Association, and the International Reading Association.

Beautiful illustrations and superb full-color photographs combine with engaging, easy-to-read stories to offer a fresh approach to each subject in the series. Each DK READER is guaranteed to capture a child's interest while developing his or her reading skills, general knowledge, and love of reading.

The five levels of DK READERS are aimed at different reading abilities, enabling you to choose the books that are exactly right for your child:

Pre-level 1: Learning to read
Level 1: Beginning to read
Level 2: Beginning to read alone
Level 3: Reading alone
Level 4: Proficient readers

The "normal" age at which a child begins to read can be anywhere from three to eight years old. Adult participation through the lower levels is very helpful for providing encouragement, discussing storylines, and sounding out unfamiliar words.

No matter which level you select, you can be sure that you are helping your child learn to read, then read to learn!

LONDON, NEW YORK, MUNICH,
MELBOURNE, AND DELHI

Editorial Lead Heather Jones
DTP Designer David McDonald
Senior Production Controller Rachel Lloyd
Associate Publisher Nigel Duffield

Reading Consultant
Linda Gambrell, Ph.D.

Produced by
Shoreline Publishing Group LLC
President James Buckley, Jr.
Designer Tom Carling, carlingdesign.com

The Boy Scouts of America®, Cub Scouts®,
Boys' Life®, and rank insignia are registered
trademarks of the Boy Scouts of America.
Printed under license from the
Boy Scouts of America.

First American Edition, 2011
11 12 13 14 10 9 8 7 6 5 4 3 2 1
Published in the United States by DK Publishing
375 Hudson Street, New York, New York 10014

Published in Great Britain by Dorling Kindersley Limited

DK books are available at special discounts when purchased in bulk
for sales promotions, premiums, fund-raising, or educational use.
For details, contact:
DK Publishing Special Markets, 375 Hudson St., New York, NY 10014
SpecialSales@dk.com

A catalog record for this book is available
from the Library of Congress.
ISBN: 978-0-7566-5037-7

Printed and bound in China by L. Rex Printing Company

The publisher would like to thank the following for their kind
permission to reproduce their photographs:
(Key: a=above; b=below/bottom; c=center; l=left; r=right; t=top)

Peter Arnold Inc.: 38r; AP/Wide World: 19b, 29t, 33b, 35b, 44r; Ralph Clevenger/
Wild Shot: 28t; Corbis: 20t, 42t; Dreamstime.com (photographers listed): Ashwin
Abhirama 20b, Mike Brown 37r, Burtet 39b, Chris Davis 44t, Vito Folefante 45b,
Jxpfeer 32b, Rosen Litov 29b, MV 32, Renata Micallef 24b, Nikolai Sorokin 4t;
iStock: 5b, 5t, 8b, 14t, 15t, 22t, 23b, 25t, 25b, 29b, 37, 40t, 41, 42b, 45t;
North Wind Pictures: 9; Photos.com: 7b, 8t, 12b, 15b, 17b, 27t

All other images © Dorling Kindersley Limited.
For more see: www.dkimages.com

Discover more at
www.dk.com

Contents

PROFICIENT
4
READERS

Boys' Life SERIES

Dangerous
Beasts

Written by James Buckley, Jr.

DK Publishing

How dangerous?

Animals of all shapes and sizes are a vital part of our world. They help us, they befriend us, they feed us. They brighten our lives as pets and they thrill us with their wide variety. From the tiniest bugs to the largest mammals, animals connect with people around the world.

Some of those connections, though, don't work as well as others. Most are wild animals, after all, and when we enter their worlds, we're just another animal. To defend themselves (or to have lunch), some animals attack humans. These are scary moments and can be dangerous. Thousands of people each year are injured or killed by animals of many kinds.

However, by learning more about these animals and how they

The numbers
How did we decide which animals to include? The main thing was how many attacks on people were reported. We looked at many places to find those numbers. None are exact. Most are estimates. But we tried to find as much about those numbers as we could before using them in this book.

live their lives, perhaps we can reduce those attacks. We share this planet with them. Perhaps if we knew more about them, we could avoid many of these attacks. The more we know, the safer we—and the animals—can be.

CAUTION
----- -----
ANIMALS
BITE

Don't worry
Unless you live in a snake- and spider-infested jungle, the chances are very, very, very small that you'll ever have to worry about the beasts in this book. But, as the saying goes, be prepared!

Not pets!
Tame house pets like cats and dogs are very safe. You must still treat them kindly, however, and respect their different needs and abilities.

Coyotes
Coyotes are not big cats, but more like big dogs. They live all over the United States. They are very shy of people, but have been known to attack house pets like cats and small dogs.

Other names
Mountain lions go by many names, including cougar, catamount, or puma.

Big cats

Next time you play with your little kitten, remember that in his mind, he is a fierce jungle cat. Though he looks like he's playing, he's really pretending you're a tasty antelope. Don't worry, though, you're still quite safe with him.

However, the same is not true of real-life big cats. Almost all of them can be very dangerous to meet in the wild. It would be more

dangerous if you were an antelope, but big cats have attacked people.

The big cat you're most likely to see in the wild is a mountain lion. These cats live in many places across the United States and Canada. As houses and parks edge into the mountain lions' territory, meetings with people increase. Though their name says "mountain," some of these cats live in swamps, forests, and parks.

They're not the biggest of the big cats. They measure 3.25 to 5.25 ft (1 to 1.6 m) long and weigh about 140 pounds (62 kg). They can be very fierce when cornered, however. When they attack people, it is usually when a hiker surprises a mountain lion on a trail. About a dozen such attacks are reported every year, but they are rarely fatal.

Puma cub
Most mountain lions are tan in color, but some species have stripes or spots as cubs.

Avoiding them
Don't hike alone. Avoid hiking very early in the morning, when the cats are likely to be eating. As you hike, make some noise to let them know you're coming.

Jaguars
Smaller but similar to tigers, jaguars used to roam most of the Americas. However, today they are quite rare. They live mostly in South America.

Masks
Some villagers try to stop attacks by wearing masks on the back of their heads to scare away tigers.

Tigers are some of the most beautiful and powerful cats in the world. They live in India and Southeast Asia (not in Africa!). A tiger's beautiful fur has familiar orange-and-black markings. That fur has led to them being hunted for centuries, as people wanted to use ther skins for clothing, furniture, and other things.

Because of this, tigers are usually very shy and don't want to meet up with humans. However, they do attack people. Villagers in India know to be very careful when walking in the jungle. Tigers that attack usually can't find other food or they are too sick to hunt animals faster than they are. In a part of northern India, many tigers were forced from the jungle following a cyclone in 2007. Attacks on people increased in that area for a time.

When an Indian villager is killed by a tiger, many times the villagers will hunt for that tiger. Often they will kill several tigers— but they're never sure if they got the "right" one.

Tigers can hurt and kill people. However, as we'll see with other animals, tigers are in much more danger from us. Most species are endangered. Many countries are working to help protect these big cats from hunters and poachers.

Have you ever heard the expression "man-eating lion"? It's true. Stories of lions attacking people have been around as long as Europeans have been traveling to Africa. In 1898, a group of lions killed more than 20 railroad workers. A pride, or group, of lions killed nearly 1,000 people near Njombe in Tanzania in the 1940s. More recently, more than 500 people have been attacked in Tanzania.

Why do lions attack humans? Usually, it's because the humans are on the lions' territory. Lions don't recognize borders or villages or lines on maps. If you're in their way, you're just an antelope on two legs. As people spread out, lions have had less and less territory in which to roam.

Really big cats
Male lions can weigh more than 350 pounds (159 kg). They have enormous teeth and huge paws. Female lions (above) are smaller, but actually fiercer.

Help for lions
Several groups in Africa, such as the Lion Conservation Project and Project Simba, are trying to help save lions by telling more people about them.

Big danger

Elephants, the largest land mammals, can also be among the most dangerous. Elephants have

Tusks
Elephant tusks are made of ivory. Thousands of elephants have been killed by poachers just to get this valuable ivory.

Baby elephants
Elephants live with their mothers for up to 10 years. Some experts say that part of the reason elephants seem to attack more may be that many mother-son pairs are being split up by hunting.

been blamed for hundreds of human deaths in just the past couple of decades. Some reports say that elephants are even more dangerous now than ever. They have rampaged through villages in India and Africa. They have attacked tourists and farm workers, as well as safari vehicles.

Why are elephants so dangerous? They do not attack humans to eat them, as lions or tigers do. Elephants are vegetarians. Some experts believe that the elephants are getting back at people for harming other elephants. The elephants might also be frustrated because humans are taking over much of their territory. Some elephants who attack people are being held captive.

Whatever the reasons, elephants and human beings are in conflict more than ever before.

Not always dangerous
How are elephants put to work? Some work in logging, moving large trees. Others carry safari visitors. Elephants are also trained to play polo or soccer.

India
Most of the recent attacks by elephants have happened in India, where humans and elephants live closer together than they do in Africa.

The hippopotamus is another large animal that has attacked humans. Like elephants, they do not attack people for food, but rather because they feel threatened. With more and more people going on safaris in places where hippos live, they have clashed with people often. They are regarded as one of the most dangerous animals in Africa, with hundreds of deaths blamed on them.

Hippos are enormous, of course, weighing more than 3,000 to 4,000 pounds (1,500 to 1,800 kg). They can also move very fast. An African gamekeeper once sprinted 100 yards to escape a charging hippo.

They are most dangerous when you are between them and their homes in or near the water. If the

Charge!
Many hippo attacks come when the animals knock into boats floating on a river or stream.

Close relative
Believe it or not, hippos are closely related to horses. Their name comes from Greek words that mean "river horse."

hippo is on land feeding and a person walks between a river and a hippo, the hippo might charge to get to the water. They have large, sharp teeth, so watch out!

Hippo birds
Pictures of hippos often show birds perched on their backs. These birds eat bugs that swarm around hippos or use the hippos as platforms to search for fish.

Why flat teeth?
Though a hippo has large, pointed teeth up front, most of its teeth are flat. This is to help them grind the grasses that make up most of their diet.

Big paws
A bear can do a lot of damage to a beehive—or a person—with its large, hand-like paws.

Snack time
Bears and humans interact when people don't keep their food hidden away from bears at campsites.

Bears are the kings of the forests they live in. Sometimes, people want to use the forests, too, and the bears react. About 20 people per decade have been killed by bears in the past hundred years in North America. Many attacks came when people surprised bears feeding in the woods, often with their cubs. Other attacks came as bears searched for food in camps or homes near forest areas.

Black bears and brown bears, including grizzlies, both have taken part in these attacks. Bears are very large and can stand more than eight feet (1.8 m) tall and weigh more

More bear tips
• Don't sleep in clothes you cooked in. They'll smell like food.
• Don't bring dogs on hikes.
• Don't run if you see a bear; stay calm and move slowly away.

Polar bears
According to Polar Bear International, only eight people have been killed by polar bears in Canada and the U.S. (Plus 19 in Russia.) They are shy and usually leave people alone.

than 600 pounds (270 kg). They have giant claws and sharp teeth.

However, hikers and campers can take precautions to avoid bears. Make sure food is stored away from tents. Metal garbage containers need to be locked. Make noise as you hike to warn bears ahead of you. Always hike in a group. Bears can be dangerous, but it's their forest, too.

Rain day
Watch out for snakes after a rainstorm. They'll be leaving their wet homes seeking higher, dryer ground.

Rattles
A rattlesnake's rattle gets larger and longer as the snake gets older.

Scary snakes

More people are afraid of snakes than any other animal. Yes, snakes can be dangerous. There are hundreds of types whose venom can harm humans. In fact, some experts think as many as 25,000 people die from snake bites each year, though most of those are in India.

However, most snakes are not dangerous. The key is knowing which kind can hurt you and how to avoid them. The easiest way is to know where snakes like to live.

In North America, there are only a few types of harmful snakes. The snakes most likely to bite people are Eastern or Western diamondback rattlesnakes. About 8,000 people are bitten by these snakes each year (many victims are people who work with snakes). However, only about a dozen people die from the bites. Experts say most bites are "dry"; that is, they do not inject venom.

The spread of people into desert and mountain areas has put people and snakes closer together. When most snakes bite people, they are just defending themselves or have been startled. Making noise and being aware on the trail is the best way to avoid snake danger.

How fangs work
Snake fangs are hollow. The fang goes into the victim and then the venom comes out of the point of the fang into the bite.

Snakebite help
The best treatment for serious bites is medicine made from snake venom. Venom "milked" from snakes is used to make an "antivenom" that helps counteract the venom's effects.

Deadly
The saw-scaled viper, which lives in India, is one of the world's deadliest snakes.

Cleopatra
This famous Egyptian queen supposedly met her end when she was bitten by an asp, a type of viper.

What are the world's deadliest snakes? Experts actually disagree about the answer to that question.

One reason is that experts have different ways of measuring how powerful or deadly a snake's venom is. For example, the krait's bite is very deadly, but it rarely bites people. So is it more dangerous than a cobra, whose bite is less dangerous but more common?

Some experts measure a snake's danger by how much venom it puts out. The king brown snake can put out .04 ounces (1,300 mg).

One thing is certain—the deadliest snakes live far from North America. Saw-scaled vipers that live in and near India kill more people than any other snake. Cobras also kill thousands.

Russell's viper is the leading killer on the island of Sri Lanka. Black mambas and boomslangs cause many deaths in Africa.

Nature has given snakes fangs and venom to defend themselves and capture prey. If people leave snakes alone, then snakes will (almost always) leave people alone.

Big and deadly
The king cobra is the largest venomous snake. They can be as long as 16 feet (5 m). One bite can kill 20 people. Or an elephant, whoever is unluckiest.

Webs
Spiders spin webs, of course, so a good way to avoid any dangerous spiders is to avoid disturbing their webs.

Bad peel
The wandering spider is sometimes called the banana spider because they often hide amid bunches of the yellow fruit.

Attack of the spiders

As with snakes, picking which spider is the most dangerous to humans is not an exact science. There are more than 40,000 species of spider, and all of them bite. However, only about a few of them are dangerous to human beings.

Two spiders that get a lot of the votes for most dangerous are the Brazilian wandering spider and the funnel-web spider. The *Guinness*

Brazilian wandering spider

Funnel-web spider

Okay for Fido
While funnel-web spider bites can seriously hurt people, most dogs and cats do not seem affected if bitten. Most bites occur in summer when male spiders are looking for mates.

Book of World Records calls the Brazilian wandering spider the world's most poisonous. However, other experts say that since its bite is so rare, its reputation is worse than reality. The bite of the funnel-web spider has been known to kill people. However, no one has died from its nasty bite since antivenom was created in 1981.

The point is that spider bites are very rare and deaths from spider bites, while real, are also very rare.

Spider teeth
All spiders have fangs or teeth. All spiders are also carnivorous, which means they eat meat.

Black widow

Closer to home in North America, two other spiders get a lot of attention for their bites. The black widow spider has earned a name for itself as being very deadly—but it's not. It rarely bites people, and its venom can make a person very sick. However, nearly all victims recover. Only a tiny handful of people have died from black widow bites. Also, most were bitten almost by accident, such as if they sat on the spider or reached into its web by mistake.

The brown recluse spider can do some serious damage to humans. Their bite can cause a reaction on skin that can be very painful. In very rare cases, someone who is bitten will need to have that skin or part of their body near the bite removed. However, as its name says, this spider is very, very shy. "Recluse" means someone (or something) that wants to stay far away from people.

What about tarantulas? Some people keep tarantula spiders as pets. Isn't that dangerous? Well, yes and no. Yes, they do bite. But if handled properly and safely, they won't hurt people.

Brown recluse

Stinging scorpions

Scorpions are related to spiders and pack a nasty sting themselves. Instead of biting, they inject their poison with a stinger at the end of their tail. Of the 2,000 species, only 30 or 40 are dangerous to people. Scorpions live mostly in desert areas. They burrow into the sand in the heat of the day and come out at night to feed on insects. They can be from about two to eight inches (6–21 cm) long.

Some sources say scorpions kill more than 1,000 people per year,

Blacklight glow
This is cool. Scorpion's bodies glow under ultraviolet light. Special lamps that shine this light make the scorpions show up bright blue even in the darkest night.

Parts
Like spiders, scorpions have eight legs. They also have two large claws. At the end of their long tail is a stinger called a "telson."

including many in Mexico (though four people have died from scorpion stings in the United States in the past decade). Other species of scorpion cause deaths in Africa and Asia.

Scorpions can be avoided, however, by watching where you walk when hiking and carefully shaking out clothing and shoes before putting them on in the morning.

Empty your shoes
When traveling in desert areas, always check your shoes before putting them on. Scorpions like cool, dark places and have been known to climb into empty shoes while people sleep.

Scorpio
This sign of the Zodiac is named for a scorpion. Scorpio is October 24 to November 22.

Diving with sharks
To take close-up pictures like these, photographers are lowered into the water in small, steel cages.

Pointy!
Shark teeth are shaped like triangles. Sharks are always growing teeth. They might have several rows of dagger-like teeth.

Sea danger

Great white sharks are feared as the deadliest creatures in the sea. That's true if you're a fish or a seal, but not if you're a person. The chances of being attacked by a great white are very, very small. In fact, most records count fewer than 100 people who have died in single attacks in the past century. (Some events, such as shipwrecks, have been the scene of larger attacks.) However, thanks to movies like *Jaws*, and the scary nature of the great white, their reputation is much worse than they deserve.

Still, they are great hunters. Their enormous size (about 4,000 pounds/1,600 kg and more than 20 ft/6m long) and their massive jaws make them eating machines. They normally attack seals, sea lions, and larger ocean fish. Human beings are nearly always attacked by mistake. The great whites think a swimming human is a tasty seal. In most attacks, they will take one bite before realizing their mistake and swimming away.

Tasty board
Sometimes sharks bite surfboards— and surfers. The bite marks on the board show how wide a shark's mouth can be!

Omnivores
Tiger sharks will eat just about anything— crabs, seals, fish, lobsters, birds, and other sharks. They have also been caught with large amounts of human trash and garbage in their stomachs.

Tiger shark

Great whites are not the only sharks that are known to attack humans. Tiger sharks are smaller and perhaps a bit quicker than great white sharks. Tiger sharks are often found in shallower waters close to shore, where they are more likely to meet up with humans. Like great whites, tiger sharks are not hunting humans, but seals or other fish.

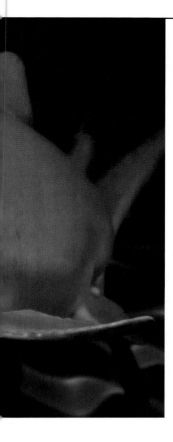

Human beings just sometimes get in the way.

Surfers are in particular danger from tiger sharks. Lying on their boards, surfers look like seals. Tiger sharks dart in, take a bite, and swim off. They discover that they won't have seal for lunch. Unfortunately, that one bite can be fatal to the person. However, fast work by rescuers can save a person who has been bitten.

Danger seals?
Seals and sea lions are normally harmless and curious. But some swimmers and divers have reported being chased, bitten, or bumped by seals, especially near shorelines.

Lucky girl
Bethany Hamilton was surfing in Hawaii one day. She was attacked by a tiger shark and lost an arm. However, she has recovered and still surfs.

Sharks are not the only fish that can be deadly to human beings. People exploring Australia's beautiful reefs have to be careful what they touch. That bumpy-looking rock might just be a deadly stonefish. Each year, dozens of people step on these fish as they hide on the bottom. The people's feet step on the fish's sharp spines, which are coated with a dangerous

Urchin spines
Painful but not deadly, urchin spines often end up in people's feet. Swimmers step on these animals when they move over reefs.

Stonefish

Blue-ringed octopus

Scared! The blue rings on this octopus only show up when the animal is startled or frightened.

Steve Irwin The TV star known as the Crocodile Hunter was killed in 2006 by a stingray. The animal's spiny tail jabbed Irwin in the chest as he swam over it. Though it was deadly in this case, stingray attacks are very, very rare.

poison. If not treated quickly, the poison can kill or seriously injure a person.

Another Australian danger is the blue-ringed octopus. Its sharp beak can inflict a nasty bite with a dangerous poison. They're just a few inches across, but the bright colors make it easy to spot—and avoid!

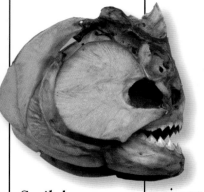

Smile!
This piranha skull gives you a good look at the many tiny, but super-sharp teeth in the jaw of a piranha. Villagers use the teeth to make sharp tools and weapons.

Long and toothy
Fishermen who hook the hard-fighting barracuda are extra careful bringing in these fish. Armed with rows of razor-teeth, the 'cuda lives in tropical waters.

One of the scariest fish in the world's waters is small enough to pick up in your hand—but you probably don't want to!

You have to travel up a steamy river in South America to cross paths with the toothy piranha. This fish has a nasty reputation as one of the fiercest aquatic biters around.

The piranha is only a few inches long when full-grown. It has a powerful jaw with many tiny but super-sharp teeth.

Thanks to cartoons and stories, piranhas are thought of as extremely

dangerous. The stories tell of a school of piranha tearing a cow to pieces in a wild eating frenzy. While it's a good story, it's not really true.

Yes, piranha do eat flesh—fish, small mammals, reptiles—and they do bite humans and other animals who wander into their river homes. However, they don't act as crazy as they do in cartoons!

Piranha also don't school tightly together except in the dry seasons, when water levels are low.

One tough fish
This red-bellied piranha is one of more than 20 species of the fish. However, this particular species is considered the most aggressive.

Gator or croc?
Two easy ways to know if an animal is a croc or a gator:
• Alligator jaws are more U-shaped. Crocodile jaws often look more like a V (above).
• A croc's fourth tooth (from the front) sticks out when its mouth is closed. An alligator covers all its teeth.

Watery danger can be found in rivers and lakes, too. In tropical climates in Asia and Australia, one of the most powerful hunters is the saltwater crocodile. This surprisingly fast animal has grabbed people from boats or pulled them from river banks. Attacks are rare, but they do happen and will keep happening when people and crocs collide.

Alligators are usually smaller than crocodiles. They live in or near rivers, swamps, and ponds. In populated, tropical areas such as Florida, alligators and humans come into contact. The state of Florida reports about a dozen attacks each year by alligators. A few such attacks end in a person's death, unfortunately. Local governments work hard to educate people about the dangers of alligators living near their communities.

Watch out!
Saltwater crocs can move very quickly and leap from the water to snare their prey.

Golf course crocs
In Florida, many golf courses have lakes or ponds. In some cases, these "water hazards" also are home to crocs or gators. Golfers have to be careful, especially when searching for lost balls near the water!

Don't do it!
A popular story says that the best way to treat a minor jellyfish sting is with urine. What actually works best is vinegar.
The acid in the vinegar calms the stinging pain.

Poison frogs
Poison dart frogs live in rain forests. Poison comes out of their skin. Local hunters use the poison on the tips of their hunting darts.

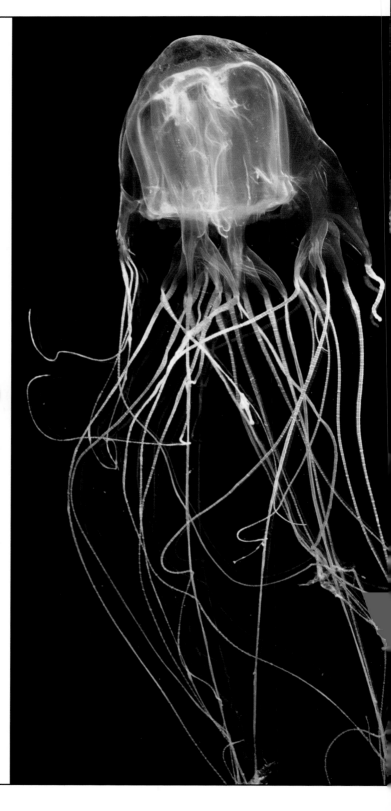

Floating quietly off the shore of Australia, the box jellyfish is just minding its own business. It's so simple, it really doesn't even have a brain. So you can't really blame it for all the trouble it causes. Also known as a sea wasp, the box jelly's long, stringing tentacles can be very dangerous to fish, sea mammals, and people. Swimmers in Australia have died after being stung once or more by these silent floaters.

The Portuguese man-of-war is another jellyfish. It lives in many places around the world. It also has long tentacles, but its poison is not deadly to humans. The man-of-war's stings are very painful, though, and should be treated right away.

Zap!
Cartoons make the electric eel look more dangerous than it is. It does use an electrical charge to stun its prey, but the charge is not enough to seriously hurt an adult person.

Slithery
Divers in the Indian and Western Pacific oceans must watch out for the banded sea snake. Though shy, this snake packs a deadly bite.

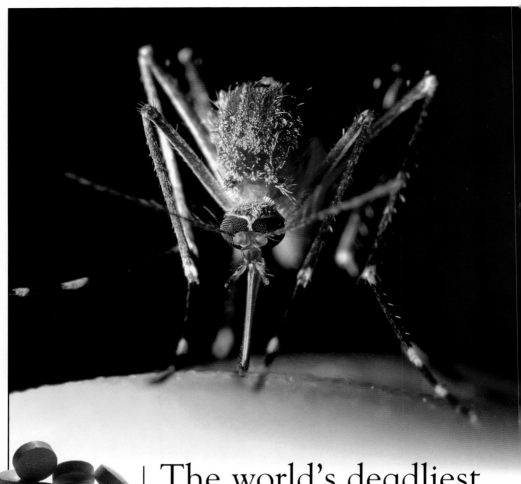

Malaria cure
Quinine is
a treatment
for malaria.
However, it
is not always
effective and
is not always
available in
remote or
poor areas.

The world's deadliest

We've traveled throughout
the animal kingdom looking at
the many types of creatures that
can cause harm to humans. They
include mammals, reptiles, and
fish. Now we come to the most
dangerous beast in the world. This
animal is responsible for the deaths

of more people than all the other animals combined—and then some. Some experts blame this animal for the deaths of millions of people each year. Oddly, this animal can be defeated more easily than just about any other, too.

The world's deadliest creature is—the mosquito.

The bite of this tiny insect spreads a disease called malaria, which kills more than two million people, mostly in Africa and Asia, each year. Female mosquitos land on a person and suck out a little blood with a long mouth probe. As they do so, they leave behind saliva that often carries malaria. In North America, mosquitos can spread West Nile virus and other illnesses. Many communities use sprays and other methods to keep mosquitos away.

Safe repellents
Instead of powerful chemicals, try natural oils like eucalyptus, citronella, lemongrass, cedar, or clove to chase away mosquitos.

Net work
Many charities raise money to buy mosquito nets to protect people sleeping in African villages. These nets can save thousands of people from being bitten.

Other insects bother people, too. Millions of people are stung by bees each year. For most people, it's just a small pain and they are not seriously injured. However, a few people get very sick or die from these bites. Those people are allergic to bee stings. This means that the venom of the stinger reacts with their bodies in

Honey bees

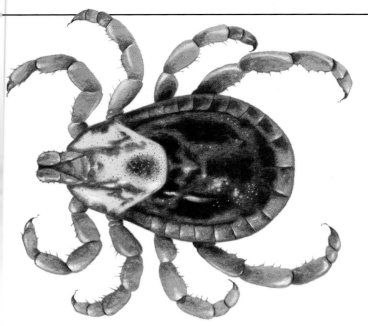

Tick

a dangerous way. The venom can make them unable to breathe. Doctors and hospitals are very good at treating such allergic reactions.

Ticks are another insect that can harm people. Like mosquitos, they spread disease. The most common is called Lyme disease. This can make some people very sick and can last for a long time. A good way to avoid being bitten by ticks is to wear long pants and high socks while hiking.

Yuck!
After you get back from a hike, check your skin carefully for ticks. If you find them, remove them with tweezers to make sure you get the entire head and body.

Killer bees
A rare type of bee called the Africanized honeybee sometimes attacks people in swarms, stinging them thousands of times. They have caused a few deaths worldwide.

Shark fin soup
Thousands of sharks are killed each year just for their fins, which are used in a popular Asian soup.

Ivory trade
Police around the world help fight people who sell illegal ivory, or elephant tusks. Here, officers show ivory captured from smugglers.

Most dangerous of all?

If you add up the numbers, humans are doing much more damage to other animals than animals are doing to us. That's not counting the animals raised for

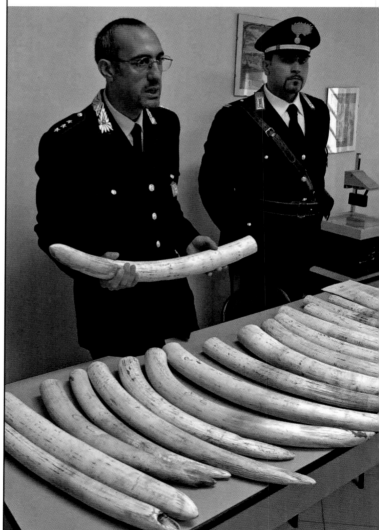

food. But looking just at the dangerous animals in this book, we're harming them more than they're harming us. That includes destruction of habitat, hunting, or removing food sources. While it's important to learn more about the dangers posed by some animals, we should also understand what we're doing to them.

We've left one animal off the "dangerous animals" list. To discover an example of this final animal, look in a mirror. Human beings cause more deaths of other humans than all the animals in the world put together. Being nicer to our fellow human animals should be our first step. We share this world with six billion people—and all the other creatures of the world, too. It's the only world we've got.

Rain forest destruction
Millions of acres of rain forest are burned each year to make more and more farmland in South America.

Tiger tale
In the 20th century, hunters reduced the world's tiger population from millions to only a few thousand.

Find out more

Books

Big Cats and Wild Dogs
By Jen Green (Southmark, 2007)
Pounce on this book if you want to find out more about lions, tigers, cheetahs, mountain lions, and even coyotes.

Crocodiles and Alligators
By John Wexo (Wildlife Eduction, 2003)
Short and sweet, this photo-packed book covers the habitats, physical features, and diets of these leftover prehistoric animals.

Eyewitness Sharks
By Miranda McQuitty (DK Publishing, 2004)
From great whites to tiger sharks, from nurse sharks to whale sharks, this book features everything you need to know about these amazing—if dangerous—creatures.

The New Encyclopedia of Snakes
By Chris Mattison
(Princeton University Press, 2007)
A world-famous snake expert takes you on a trip through this slithery world. The book includes hundreds of colorful, close-up pictures.

Web sites

Animal Planet
**animal.discovery.com/convergence/oceans-deadliest/
deadliest-creatures.html**
This cable channel has a Web site with tons of animal
info. This section highlights facts about dangerous
ocean creatures.

National Geographic
animals.nationalgeographic.com/animals
Use this famous site's "Animals A-Z" search tool to find out
facts and see pictures of hundreds of animals, both dangerous
and safe!

Rattlesnakes
Rattlesnakes.com
Visit the home of the American International Rattlesnake
Museum in New Mexico. You can see pictures of their
exhibits and learn facts about rattlers and other snakes.

More about sharks
http://www.flmnh.ufl.edu/fish/Kids/kids.htm
The Florida Museum of Natural History has a kids-only
section with stories, links, videos, photos, and more, all about
sharks and other amazing fish.

*Note to Parents: These Web sites are not endorsed by Boy Scouts of America or DK Publishing and have
not been completely examined. However, at press time, they provided the sort of information described.
Internet experts always suggest that you work with your children to help them understand how to safely
navigate the Web.*

Glossary

Allergic
Having a dangerous reaction to something that can cause pain or even death.

Antivenom
Medicine used to treat snake bites.

Aquatic
Having to do with the water.

Carnivorous
Eating only meat.

Conflict
A disagreement, fight, or battle.

Cyclone
A very serious storm occurring in the Southern Hemisphere, with high winds and heavy rain.

Estimates
Educated guesses based on facts and real information.

Fatal
Causing death.

Frenzy
A wild and uncontrolled outburst.

Habitat
The area in which an animal usually lives.

Infested
Filled, overwhelmed with.

Malaria
A blood disease of the tropics that causes high fever, breathing problems, and death.

Milking
Extracting venom from a snake by forcing it out of its fangs into a container.

Precautions
Preparations against a possible problem.

Pride
In this case, a group of lions.

Quinine
A medicine made from cinchona trees that is used to treat malaria.

Recluse
A person who chooses to live away from other people.

Repellents
Substances that chase away bugs or prevent them from stinging.

Safaris
Trips, usually in Africa, on which visitors see wildlife.

Smugglers
Criminals who carry illegal goods across national borders.

Species
Types of animals.

Spines
Sharp, pointy body parts of some animals.

Tentacles
Long, dangling arms belonging to jellyfish.

Ultraviolet light
An invisible type of light that can reveal certain types of animals or substances not seen with normal light.

Vegetarian
A person or animal that eats only plant matter.

Venom
A poisonous substance that is put out by snakes when they bite.